Crikey I'm... ™

A Dad

Other titles in the *Crikey I'm...* **series**

Crikey I'm...™

A Dad

Contributors

Dr David Haslam
Victoria Warner
Eliza Williams

Edited by

Steve Hare

Cover Illustration by

Ian Pollock

PURPLE HOUSE

Published by Purple House Limited 1998
75 Banbury Road
Oxford OX2 6PE

© Purple House Limited 1998

Cover illustration: © Ian Pollock/The Inkshed

Crikey I'm... is a trademark of Purple House
Limited

A catalogue record for this book is available
from the British Library

ISBN 1-84118-017-3

Printed in Great Britain by
Cox and Wyman

Acknowledgements

We are grateful to everyone who helped in the compilation of this book, particularly to the following:

Stephen Franks of Franks and Franks (Design)

Inform Group Worldwide (Reproduction)

Dave Kent of the Kobal Collection

Parents at Work

Office of National Statistics

Bodleian Library, Oxford

Central Library, Oxford

British Film Institute

Liz Brown

Mark McClintock

Hannah Wren

Illustrations

Contents

Crikey, I'm A Dad!

When you were born, it was entirely likely that your father was excluded from what should have been the most intense experience of his life. All this has changed radically in a very short space of time. From the 1980s more than 90 per cent of all fathers – more than half a million each year – have been present at the birth of their children.

In that time an insidious preconception – reinforced in thousands of cartoons, situation comedies, advertisements, jokes and books – has been gradually eroded. The father-figure, out at work all day, dispenser of discipline (just wait till your father gets home) and little else, has been replaced by a caring, sharing 'new man'.

Today's father has been involved throughout, sharing the experience at ante-natal classes, viewing scans, and marvelling at the amazing elastic properties of their partner's body, and the internal acrobatics. Powerful taboo kept primitive man, with few exceptions, apart from his wife throughout pregnancy, often until the baby could crawl.

That process continues today. In only four per cent of households is the wife the sole breadwinner. In more than 80 per cent, the father is in full-time employment. Paternity leave is still relatively uncommon. It is maintained that fathers spend an average of eight minutes a day with their children. Eight minutes.

More than half of all male adults still believe that it is a husband's job to earn money, and a wife's to look after the family. The percentage of women concurring with that sentiment is not much lower. But the father who changes nappies, gets up in the night, bottle-feeds and helps with the housework is no longer sneered at or frowned upon but, rather, universally admired. And in their turn, your children will learn from your example.

Motherhood, we are told, is an instinct; where that falls short, there are countless books to refer to, and mothers to defer to. Fatherhood is an altogether less concrete concept. It is a role you can make your own.

Forefathers

Fatherhood Through History

There must have been a time in our ancient past when the sex act and the birth of a baby some nine months later were viewed as quite separate and unrelated occurrences. People walked, sat, ate, defecated, killed, had babies. One act did not cause the other. Plants died and new ones appeared in the spring. Animals and birds had young. The sun rose each morning and died again each night. Miracles happened.

In primitive times the life expectancy of men and women was not great: surviving to their mid thirties was a real achievement. But then, unlike today, it was the men who lived longer. Men might face the daily dangers of wild animals, marauding raiders and battle; but women had the rigours of recurrent childbirth to contend with. For the primitive mother, raising children was in itself a full-time occupation, with agriculture, animal husbandry and cooking no doubt thrown in for good measure. And the constant round of pregnancy, birth and care would inevitably take its toll. The men might be broken, but the women just wore out.

Changing Roles of the Father

'The father should normally be the wage earner, the person who comes and goes and brings prosperity and adventure into the home.'

From *The Art of Marriage*,
Mary Macaulay, Penguin, 1952

In the earliest cultures, where the nuclear family was unknown,

All together now – James Stewart and family in *It's A Wonderful Life*, 1946.

women possessed a power and status in their societies that they have only begun to win back this century. There could only ever be certainty about the mother of any child; the father could be any of the males with whom she associated. And it was the mother, caring for her children, who possessed the power of life or death over those children and thus the success and survival of the group to which she belonged. The earliest gods were women, with goddesses representing motherhood and the miracle of regeneration.

> 'Wrinkles are hereditary. Parents get them from their children.'
>
> Doris Day

By the time history came to be recorded in writing, rather than through surviving artefacts and cave paintings, society, in just about every country, was organised around men, and women were relegated to an inferior status, often only one step above actual slavery. The most powerful gods had become male, too.

It is the act of fathering, rather than the sympathetic portrayal of fatherhood, that figures strongly in Greek and Roman mythology. Zeus had an odd relationship with his own father. His mother Rhea only prevented her husband Kronos from swallowing her baby by giving him a boulder wrapped in swaddling clothes instead. Zeus later usurped his position as chief among the gods. Despite the Greeks' monogamous outlook, Zeus was a philanderer, consorting

5

with various goddesses and mortals, to the eternal disgust and wrath of his jealous wife Hera. To escape her attentions, Zeus would adopt disguises – as a swan or bull.

Oedipus was doubly unfortunate in his parental relations, killing his father and unwittingly marrying his own mother. She hanged herself on discovering this fact, while Oedipus blinded himself, leaving four children by the incestuous relationship.

> **Children have 'traditional' views on the role of a good father. They think it is important for fathers to make and mend things around the house and make them laugh, but feel that to 'do things for you like washing and cooking' is more the role of a good mother.**
>
> From a MORI poll on children (8–15 yrs), 1997

The Bible has a lot to say on the subject, and though the New Testament is considerably more relaxed on the subject than the Old, it can still be a little hard for men and women to take literally at the end of the twentieth century: 'Wives, submit yourselves unto your own husbands, as unto the Lord. For the husband is the head of the wife, even as Christ is the head of the church: and he is the saviour of the body.'

It had been taught for generations that labour pains had originally been inflicted on women because of the

Jupiter (Zeus to the Greeks) in one of many representations, 2nd Century AD; Ashmolean Museum, Oxford.

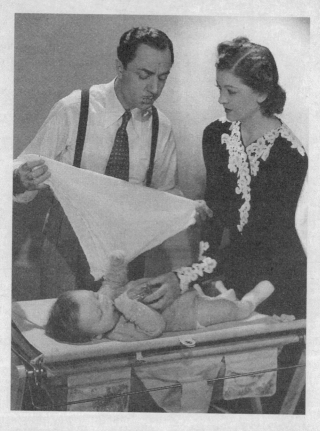

William Powell gets to grips with the basics in *Another Thin Man*, 1939.

sin of Eve in the Garden of Eden. The Fall was Eve's fault, and Adam was not slow to pass on this information, and got off rather

> **The average age to become a father for the first time in Britain is 28.**

lightly in consequence. 'I will greatly multiply thy sorrow and thy conception,' says Genesis, 'in sorrow thou shalt bring forth children; and thy desire shall be to thy husband, and he shall rule over you.' The creation of Eve herself, of course, was depicted – possibly only because of a mistranslation – as an afterthought, fashioned from a spare part of Adam.

Women in medieval Britain would typically spend the great majority of their adult lives being reminded of Eve's fallibility, bearing and rearing children, often on an almost annual basis. The ideal of a good woman was, not unnaturally, inextricably linked with motherhood. On the other hand, in the case of a childless marriage, it was always assumed that the fault must lie with the mother. Double standards reigned in matters of marital fidelity as well as impotence.

Wives and husbands depended on hearsay and guesswork, or the bizarre *Aristotle's Masterpiece*, first published in Britain in the seventeenth century and still in use during the early part of this century, despite the fact that it talked of monstrous births, and suggested that a baby with a hare-lip could only be the result of the mother meeting a hare while pregnant.

Only the most desperate and unlucky mothers gave birth alone. The majority would be attended at the very least by a neighbour. Traditionally, the husband would be nearby but never present. This was a stance that typically extended into the baby's later life, the father-figure being seen as stern and aloof, dispensing family law and discipline, too busy providing an income to become intimately involved in the daily domestic routine.

> **'By the time a man realises that maybe his father was right, he usually has a son who thinks he's wrong.'**
>
> Charles Wadsworth

Children did not necessarily stay at home or even near when they started to work, which could be at almost any age after infancy. It was common for them to be separated by some distance, only returning for special celebrations and holidays. The more wealthy parents might send their child to a monastery to learn the basic subjects and Latin.

The introduction of chloroform in the nineteenth century meant that privileged women could, once again, lie back and think of England, and play no active part in the most important moment in their lives. Yet even in the 1920s it was pointed out, to great effect, that it was four times more dangerous to bear a child than to work in a mine. The move from home births to hospital began in earnest.

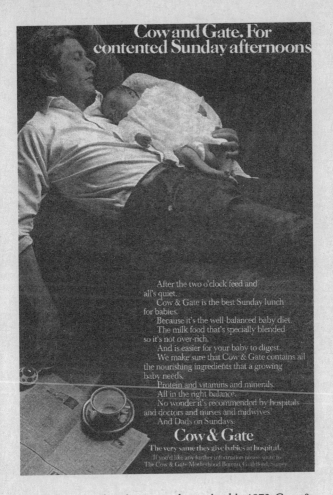

Fathering the relaxed way, as shown in this 1972 Cow & Gate advertisement.

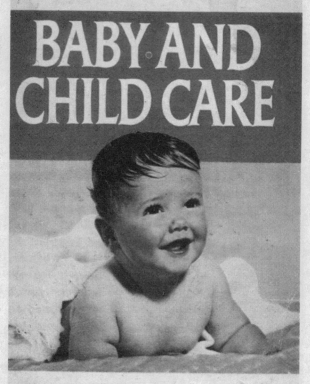

DR. BENJAMIN SPOCK

BABY AND CHILD CARE

The most widely recommended handbook for parents ever published — Authoritative, illustrated, indexed

The definitive parenting book of the fifties, first published in 1946.

The introduction of the National Health Service after World War Two, along with the availability of anti-biotics, vitamins and free orange juice for infants rapidly reduced the risks of childbirth and infant mortality. And the growing acceptance of the necessity for contraception – officially endorsed by the Church of England in 1958 – meant that parent-hood could finally be a matter of choice, rather than chance. The introduction of the contraceptive pill in the 1960s was greeted as the perfect solution – as much to liberated women as to carefree men.

> From a poll by Harris about teenagers and sex from June 1997, it was found that most British teenagers find their fathers hard to approach about their sexual worries. Three in four say they feel unable to have a conversation about such issues with their fathers.

Through the great majority of history, with few exceptions, right until the latter half of this century, childbirth has been viewed as the exclusive province of women. Films and TV dramas in the 1960s still portrayed the father nervously pacing the waiting-room floor, chain-smoking, and later distributing cigars in his local.

Today's new man, of course, is fully involved – and has eschewed all forms of smoking long since. But even if the great majority of fathers can now claim to have been present at the birth of their children, women, of course, could always claim 100 per cent involvement.

In the last decades, trad-itional and endlessly reinforced 'ideals' of the father as provider and mother as carer have gradually eroded.

With reliable contraception and the likelihood of both husband and wife locked into careers and financial commitments, parenthood today is a matter of careful planning. Ultimately though, it is still the mother in the great majority of cases who spends most time with the child.

The new man, though, is not so very new. Diaries and letters from any age will reveal deep affection, and unbounded grief at the loss of an infant on the part of a father.

At the same time, the sheer danger of childbirth and the consequent death of mothers in childbirth propelled many fathers into an unplanned domestic role.

"O-o-o-h! It's Daddy's favourite...peaches and cream!
(NESTLÉ'S, OF COURSE)"

NESTLÉ'S. In a changing world this name has always
been a guarantee of purity, unvarying quality and honest
value. This is something that three generations of British
housewives have found out for themselves. And it's a belief
fully shared by the grocers, confectioners and chemists they
buy from. Look at the famous products illustrated below.

Each one is the acknowledged best of its kind on sale
today. But Nestlé's have never been content to rest on
their reputation. They keep on searching for new ways to
improve the quality of their foods. And they never relax
their traditional high standards. Without a doubt it
is this special attitude towards food products that makes
the words *Made by Nestlé's* such a sure guide to quality.

If it's

Nestlé's

it's good...very good!

Fifties fatherhood from 1956.

15

The lengths you will go to – Bobby Vernon in *Cry Baby*, 1943.

Otherwise historical circumstances, such as employment for long hours or at distant locations, and prolonged absence during war, have conspired to add a degree of aloofness over the relationship that was never intended.

'...It is not so strange that I love you with my whole heart, for being a father is not a tie which can be ignored. Nature in her wisdom has attached the parent to the child and bound them together with a Herculean knot.'

Diary entry by
Sir Thomas More, 1517.

Paternity Leave

The concept of paternity leave remains a matter for the discretion of individual employers. The only right a father can legally claim is to take time off to attend the birth. There is a steady increase in employers granting further concessions to fathers, albeit a matter of days, rather than weeks or months. This is set to be formalised at the end of the millennium, when Britain will fall in line with an EC Directive guaranteeing three months' leave from work to both parents. Maternity leave has been available to qualifying employees since 1975.

The organisation Parents at Work argues that the cost to employers of providing paid leave to fathers will be very low: there are only 42 births per 1,000 men of working age each year. On the other hand, the employer may well see real benefits. Helping a new father both financially and in terms of time off will significantly impact on a time of genuine stress, and will ultimately produce a tangible payback in terms of reduced stress levels, morale and higher productivity.

Rupert Fawcett's 'Daddy' in a sticky situation!

BABYGRO FOR BEGINNERS

Funny things, babies.
And suddenly, you've one of your own.
You're doing things you swore to the blokes in the office you'd never do.

You're only a beginner – and that's where we come in. – Babygro.

We invented the Babygro suit.
It's an all-in-one baby outfit and we patented the stretchy cotton/'Bri-Nylon' fabric which actually grows as the baby grows.

It's got seamless shoulders, so it can't rub. We patented that too.
And the special 'Oro-Toe' foot that will never cramp would-be footballers' toes.

Ever drawn the line at washing and ironing?

Funny you should say that. Babygro machine washes, drips dry. Just like your socks.

Ever said you'd never change a nappy? Babygro poppers make it easy – Like filling in the pools.

Babygro comes in lots of colours and 3 sizes right up to 2 years. The first size with a two-way mitten cuff.

It's a man's best friend.
Suits his nature and his pocket. From 95p (19/-).
So, any father left holding the baby should remember what mother's expecting –
Nothing but the real Babygro.

Babygro
for expectant fathers

Babygro Limited,
16 Berkeley Street, London W1X 6AP. Tel: May 5834

New dads helped along by Babygro in 1971.

Different Dads

Fathers In Other Cultures

There is no across-the-board formula telling you how to be a father – the society and community into which you are born will usually govern your behaviour. In most cultures, the role of the father tends to fall into two distinct groups. This depends on whether the traditions are patrilineal or matrilineal, for it is this that determines which gender has overall authority.

Patrilineal societies are by far the most common. In these communities, the

Out in the Cold

In the Loyalty Islands it was customary for the entire population to flock to watch the birth of a child, except for the husband who alone was excluded. He then did not even visit until the baby could crawl.

biggest rituals usually symbolise the son growing into a man. Often this process will involve the son presenting his father with a token or payment for being 'allowed' to become a man. Amongst the Nuoro of Uganda, for example, the son must make a small payment to his father before performing any action that indicates manhood – such as smoking or shaving. In the community of the Tallensi of Ghana it can be extremely damning for sons to do anything that may be seen to be assuming his father's place, which can be as simple as looking into his granary!

Another peculiar occurrence of patrilineal societies can be seen amongst the Yanomamo of the South American rainforest, where it is common to marry into the same family groups generation after generation. This can create a situation where a man's wife is from the same lineage as his mother, who will then be considered his in-law.

Sons and fathers have an easier relationship in matrilineal societies where the authority over the son rests with the mother's brother. The lack of influence of the father over the child is taken to extremes amongst the people of the Trobriand Islands near Papua New Guinea, who believe that the mother is impregnated by her ancestral totemic spirit. The father and the sex act are seen to have nothing to do with pregnancy, so therefore the father is not an official relative; however he is still an important member of society.

Bobby Vernon tries to keep a low profile in *Cry Baby*, 1943.

Dennis the Menace's dad lets off steam.

Children who are born into the community of Todas Indians in Southern India will have a wide choice of fathers, as this is a polyandrous society where a wife will have many husbands. Often the husbands are all brothers; and when a child is born they are all equally responsible for it, but one will take on legal fatherhood by partaking in a 'Bow Ceremony'. In modern times, this ritual involves the relevant father presenting the mother with a plastic bow and arrow.

Although most cultures do have prescribed roles for different genders when it comes to parenting, this is not true of the Aka Pygmies who live in the African Congo. Mothers and fathers share the roles of hunting and childcare equally – the fathers have been found to be in arm's reach of or holding their children for 47 per cent of the time. Sometimes a father will allow the child to suckle his nipples for comfort, if the mother is not available.

Would you be more careful if it was you that got pregnant?

Anyone married or single can get advice on contraception from the Family Planning Associatio Margaret Pyke House, 27-35 Mortimer Street, London W1 N 8BQ. Tel. 01-636 9135.

The Family Planning Association used shock tactics on careless seventies men.

Labour Intensive

Couvade Customs

While tradition throughout history has generally dictated that fathers suffer enforced absence while their wives gave birth, the experience might still be shared in different ways. Couvade was a common custom whereby the husband simulated labour and the birth of his child. This might involve simply going to bed, or actually experiencing the pains of sympathetic labour. Such customs were still practised earlier this century. There are various theories as to the purpose of couvade. In a rather less organised society it might be a formal means of demonstrating or asserting paternity. Or, as was common with many rituals and customs, it might have originated as a ploy to distract the evil spirits who might otherwise have attacked his wife and child at this vulnerable time.

In 1993, 670,000 men became fathers. The youngest was 13 and the oldest were 75+. There were 53 in the last category!

The Victorian anthropologist Sir Everard im Thurn gave this extraordinary account of the ritual in British Guyana:

> Even before the child is born, the father abstains for a time from certain kinds of animal food. The woman works as usual up to a few hours before the birth of the child. At last she retires alone, or accompanied by some other

women, to the forest, where she ties up her hammock; and then the child is born. Then, in a few hours – often less than a day – the woman, who like all women living in a very unartificial condition, suffers but little, gets up and resumes her ordinary work. In any case, no sooner is the child born than the father takes to his hammock, and, abstaining from every sort of work, from meat and all other food, except weak gruel of cassava meal, from smoking, from washing himself, and, above all, from touching weapons of any sort, is nursed and cared for by all the women of the place. One other regulation is certainly quaint: the interesting father may not scratch himself with his finger-nails, but he may use for this purpose a splinter, specially provided, from the mid-rib of a cokerite palm. This continues for many days and sometimes even weeks.

Ten Most Popular Children's Names (1996)

1. Sophie	1. Jack
2. Jessica	2. Daniel
3. Chloe	3. Thomas
4. Emily	4. James
5. Lauren	5. Joshua
6. Rebecca	6. Matthew
7. Charlotte	7. Ryan
8. Hannah	8. Samuel
9. Amy	9. Joseph
10. Megan	10. Liam

A Fit Father

Dr David Haslam

At last you're a dad. It's wonderful, and it's terrifying. The first three months after your first baby is born will inevitably bring the greatest change to your life so far. It is wonderful, but it will be terrifying, a curious mixture of climax and anticlimax. Being a father will take you to the highest highs, but will also bring more than its fair share of anxiety and worry. You are now a dad for ever, and life will never be quite the same again.

In the first few days after the birth, you will almost certainly be incredibly busy. Don't look at any time off from work after the baby is born as being some kind of holiday, with the added bonus of a new-born baby. It will be hard work, and you will also be surprisingly nervous. This is a whole new job, and you will find yourself wondering if you can manage.

There isn't a dad alive who hasn't been scared that he is going to drop his baby, but you will never meet a dad who actually has. Despite feeling that you are all fingers and thumbs, and despite your ham-fistedness when you first change a nappy, you will cope!

New Dads: Getting Physical
- Now that you are a dad, you don't owe it only to yourself to stay fit and healthy: you owe it to your family. However, there is a real temptation to spend every evening exhausted in front of the TV – the beginning of a slippery slope to a flabby future. So

try to get three sessions a week of real exercise that you enjoy, sufficient to raise a sweat.

- If you smoke, don't. Stop now. This isn't just the usual nagging: what you do for yourself is your own business, but the simple fact is that babies whose parents smoke suffer a higher incidence of many conditions, including asthma and ear infections; and instances of cot death are also significantly higher. Can you possibly still smoke, knowing that? If you need help, talk to your doctor.

- From a strictly medical point of view, it is safe to resume sexual intercourse after about two weeks – provided any vaginal discharge has stopped, and any stitches have healed. However, the great majority of couples wait very much longer than this. Even after the bruising and discomfort caused by childbirth has eased, the sex drive is definitely reduced in many women, which could be nature's way of spreading families out. So don't forget the importance of romance, and simply cuddling and holding her. And when you do consider intercourse again, be very gentle and considerate; use a lubricant; and do make sure that your partner is as keen to make love as you are.

- Parenthood can be exhausting, not least because the little darlings have a tendency to wake at night, over and over again. Do share the night-time duties. Pretending to be asleep until your partner eventually gets up and goes to sort the baby out is just not

The breadwinner eats
more Hovis now . . .

to keep up his strength
the sensible way

Hovis THE BETTER-BALANCED BREAD

Post-war dads are urged to keep up their strength by Hovis in 1948.

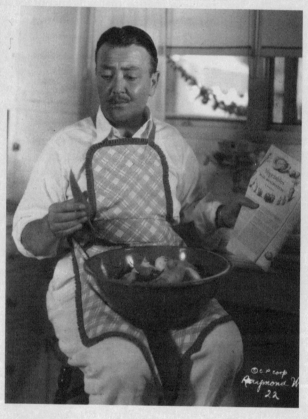

Housework doesn't come naturally to everybody!

fair. Sharing the sleeplessness will mean that you both get at least some sleep. In addition, do try to get your baby into a routine that will encourage a mutually restful sleep pattern for you and the child. Your health visitor will be able to give you advice.

New Dads: Getting Emotional

Don't worry if you don't feel overwhelming love for your new baby right from the start. Some fathers enjoy parenthood straight away, finding the whole process easy, natural and satisfying. Others have to work at it, and really only find their emotions kicking in when the baby becomes more of an individual, and less of a tiny, crying, fragile, and helpless being.

However much they have been looking forward to the baby's arrival, many men will suffer pangs of jealousy when their child arrives home. The baby will take up almost all your partner's time and attention, and, in addition, another human being is developing an incredibly close and physical relationship with her, and many men do find this genuinely troubling. And when exhaustion means that bedtime seems too precious for sex, you may feel very rejected. Talk it over. Don't keep the feelings to yourself. You are very normal, and simply talking can often greatly improve the situation..

Having a baby is extremely hard work, and your partner may be surprised by how tired she feels. In most houses, even today, there is gross inequality of division in labour when it comes to housework; so if your partner is the one who normally does the housework, remember that rest and support are much more important for both her and you than a tidy house.

For almost every mother, the 'baby blues' is normal, and typically starts on the third or fourth day after the birth. However, if after the first couple of weeks your partner continues to be constantly weepy, suffers from feelings of panic, seems unable to cope, and has little interest in her baby, you, or the home, then she may well be developing post-natal depression. This affects around five per cent of mothers, and no one is immune. It is very treatable and needs to be taken seriously, so do discuss the problem with her, and tell your GP, midwife, or health visitor right away.

These are magical times. However rich and successful you might become later in life, you will never ever be able to revisit these precious moments. It is a well-worn cliché, but it really is true that your children will grow up quicker than you would ever have believed. Enjoy this time, and do take lots of photographs, or videos.

These are, however, also stressful times. When your baby is unwell, you will be incredibly concerned, even if it is only a cold.

So as parents, you need to care for each other as well. It is vitally important that you don't take your partner or yourself for granted.

You can both pay so much attention to the baby that

you forget your own emotional needs, as individuals and as a couple.

For most men, fatherhood is the most fulfilling and wonderful experience of their lives. The birth was only the beginning. Have fun!

David Haslam is married with two children and has been a GP for 22 years. He is a Fellow of the Royal College of General Practitioners, and has written numerous books – the most recent being Stress Free Parenting. *He also writes a column for* Practical Parenting *magazine, and frequently broadcasts on health topics.*

Dream or nightmare? Men enjoy the pregnancy experience in this 1998 Britvic commercial.

Father Figures

The Myths of Fatherhood

Ever since the beginning of creation, where there has been life, there have been fathers. In terms of ancient mythology, fathers are the source of creative power, a complex role which represents the authority controlling the world, as some of the following legends point out only too clearly:

Atum

Atum was the father of all the Egyptian gods. He emerged from a waste of waters known as 'Nun'. Atum created, and vomited forth twin divinities, Shu (the god of air) and his sister-wife Tefnut (the goddess of water).

Both Atum's children, Shu and Tefnut, were cared for partly by 'Atum's Eye'. Once, when the two children were lost, Atum sent forth his Eye to seek

> **'Perhaps the greatest social service that can be rendered by anybody to the country and to mankind is to bring up a family.'**
> George Bernard Shaw

them, whilst creating a second Eye for himself. The second Eye was brighter than the first, and when the first returned it was angered to find itself outshone. Atum put it on his forehead to placate it, and it ruled the world he later created. Men associated this eye with the sun's power. Atum was eventually replaced by Ra, another famous father figure.

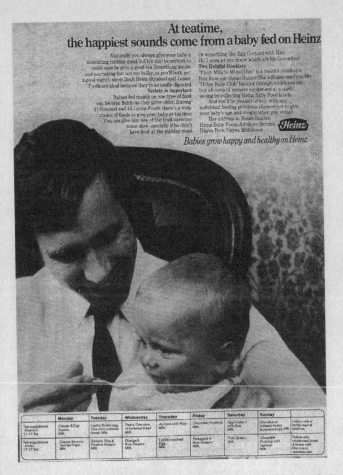

A Heinz advertisement from 1971 shows the most tender side of fatherhood.

Hercules, father of 70 children (*Hercules and the Erymanthian Boar,* c. 1576, Ashmolean Museum, Oxford).

The Daghdha

The Daghdha is a Celtic god. His name means, literally, 'good god': he is the sky-father, fertility deity and war-god.

Odin

Odin was the father of the Norse gods. He was also known as the 'All Father', and 'Father of Battle'. The son of Bor and Bestla, Odin created the world by destroying – along with his brothers Vili and Ve – the ice god Ymir. Odin was father to Thor and to Balder; some said he was also the father of Loki, the god of mischief. Two ravens and two wolves brought Odin news of the world of men, far below his seat in the heavens.

> **10% of single parents in the UK are single fathers. 25% of these are widowers.**

Heroic Coupling

Chief among the Greek gods, Zeus was somewhat less than the ideal husband and father. It was his habit to slip away to have his way with mortal women, disguised in the hope that his wife Hera would not notice. When Zeus decided to father the most renowned of Greek heroes, Hercules, he went to considerable lengths, bribing the sun not to appear for three days, and the moon to travel more slowly, so he could enjoy an extended night of passion with the mortal Alcmene, disguised as her absent husband. During her pregnancy it was obvious she was carrying the baby of a god: he was enormous, and the birth

Expectant Fathers:
Nappy changing's easy!

Read this and you'll know how.
All you do is take a Harringtons Terry Nappy
and follow these instructions. But one word
of warning; make sure it's a Harringtons Nappy.
Harringtons Nappies stay new-looking for longer.
And they're great for absorbency.
Right, start now:

1 Fold the nappy diagonally corner to corner. That's right, it's now a triangle.		**4** Fold the lower end of the nappy upwards.	
2 Lie baby on his back on the nappy.		**5** Pin together, slipping two fingers between the baby and the nappy to prevent pricking him.	
3 Bring the two outside ends of the nappy to the front.		**6** Then pull on Harringtons Baby Pants.	

'What a comfortable baby
you must be! Isn't Daddy clever!'

Harringtons

Helpful hints from Harringtons, 1958.

was certain to be difficult. It was made doubly so by the interference of Zeus's jealous wife; she sent Eileithyia, the goddess invoked by pregnant women, to sit near her, cross-legged, with her fingers intertwined – this created powerful spells to prevent childbirth.

Alcmene was sure she would not survive the ordeal, but one of her servants, Galanthis, tricked the goddess by declaring that Hercules had been safely delivered. Eileithyia sprang up, breaking the spell, and the hero was born. Galanthis, for her deception, was turned into a weasel, and because she had lied to help a woman give birth – weasel words – she was condemned to bear her own young through her mouth. The Greeks and Romans evidently believed this was how weasels bore their young! Hercules, however, started as he meant to go on, strangling two snakes, sent by the jealous Hera, while still in his cradle.

Who's the Dad?

The Nuer of Southern Sudan have a tradition whereby, if a man dies before he has married and raised a family, his younger brother must marry in his name. Any children that are born to the couple are seen as belonging to the dead man, rather than their biological father.

Agamemnon
Agamemnon shot a stag in the sacred grove of Artemis, the Greek goddess, and proclaimed himself a

better hunter than her. The goddess was angry, and Agamemnon had to promise her the first 'fruit' of his 'harvest'. This wasn't, however, a vegetable but his daughter Iphigeneia.

> 'Children are natural mimics who act like their parents despite every effort to teach them good manners.'
>
> Anon

During the Trojan war, the Greeks were prevented from disembarking at Aulis, and this was seen by one of the prophets as a sign of Artemis' anger. Agamemnon thus sent for his daughter on the pretext that she would be married to Achilles; instead of dressing her in bridal robes, however, he clothed her in sacrificial garb and placed her on the altar. In the Euripides version of the story, Artemis relented at the last moment and replaced the girl with a hind, transporting Iphigeneia to Tauris where she became a High Priestess for that goddess.

Great Father

The 'Great Father' is a Welsh god. Also called the 'Horned God' or the 'Lord', he is lord of the winter, the harvest, the dead, the sky, animals, destruction and regeneration. The great Father is the male principle of creation in ancient Welsh mythology.

Fatherly fun with William Powell in *Another Thin Man*, 1939.

Dad Ditties

1. *Daddy Bug*, Roy Ayers, 1969
2. *Daddy Does the Dishes*, Rosenshontz, 1988
3. *Daddy Don't You Tell No Lies*, Sikahn, 1989
4. *Daddy Don't You Walk So Fast*, Jimmy Jackson, 1976
5. *Daddy Flew a Spitfire*, Limey, 1977
6. *Daddy Keeps on Plowin'*, Front Porch String Band, 1992
7. *Daddy Never Was the Cadillac Kind*, Condederate Railroad, 1994
8. *Daddy the Swingin' Suburbanite*, Weird-Ohs, 1964
9. *Daddy Trane and Cousin Wayne*, Aurora, 1988
10. *Daddy Was a Communist*, Latex Generation, 1996

Copyright Notices